Echoes of My
African Mind—Griot

Prose & Poetry

by

Alf E.F. Muronda

MASAKA PUBLISHING MEDIA HOUSE

MASAKA PUBLISHING
MEDIA HOUSE

ISBN 978-1-965398-27-2   Published 2025

© Elfigio F Muronda

Published By:

MASAKA PUBLISHING MEDIA HOUSE

Harare, Zimbabwe - Cherry Hill, New Jersey

alf@cp7sisters.com

Cover Painting: VALENTINE K MUTASA

Design and all artworks by Alf E F Muronda.

Introduction

"I write to remember, and to remind the world we were never voiceless, only unheard."
Anonymous

Echoes of My African Mind – Griot is my voice, hopefully not shouting at the wind but to ride the wind, carried into the ears of those who come after me. The book is my ritual act of remembering and revealing. It seeks to carry the reflections of life, the tenderness of love, the pride of ancestry, and the fire of resistance. These poems and prose pieces arise from a spirit that has witnessed both the beauty and brutality of lived experience, as an African in the larger world and as a witness.

The volume unfolds in four parts, each a chamber of thought and memory.
"Walk A While In My Shoes" opens the journey. These 18 pieces map my inner terrain, where joy and sorrow coexist, where many of my questions echo louder than answers. Here, you'll find the voices that have walked beside me and the quiet revelations I've carried alone

"Love, Lost & Found" is a hymn to the heart coming from my experiences, both good and bad, my vulnerabilities exposed. These verses trace love's arc, its uplift, its ache, and its return. Some truths are mine. Others, I've simply witnessed.

"Griot" is an invocation of memory. In this section, I raise my pen like a talking drum, calling forth the spirits of our ancestors. This is homage, an offering to the cultural strength that carried us through slavery, colonialism, racism, and the ache of displacement. Through these poems, I honour the legacy of endurance that should guide us.

"Vignettes of War" is a tribute carved in courage. Here, I remember my brothers and countless young comrades who left childhood behind to fight for the dream of freedom. These verses speak of sacrifice and belief, of youthful fire met with the cold steel of colonial violence. They remind us that Zimbabwe's liberation was not gifted, it was claimed, fiercely, painfully, and triumphantly.

Together, these four sections form a griot's song—braided with memory, echoing the life I've lived at home and in the larger world.

Table of Contents

II   *Love, Lost & Found*   *(continued)*

III   *Griot*   *63*

IV   *Vignettes Of War*   *83*

Walk A While In My Shoes

Back Into The Cosmos We Return

We were here before,
      witnesses to the boundless night,
      woven into the fabric of infinity
          and the oneness of humanity.
      Now we return.

Before earth whispered wishes into the stars,
      I rode the wild winds of comets.
      I roamed the heavens,
      adrift in the silent embrace of creation,
      where divinity and dust became one.

Born of the swirling ether, spun into colour,
      into light woven into rainbows,
      into motion—with the first whispers of the universe,
      I emerged.

I lived the dream of the beginning
      pulsating in the womb of the mysteries of life.

I swayed in the slipstream of wandering comets,
      before earth first glimpsed falling stars.

I bathed in the waters of the gods
      in the cosmic oneness of divinity.

I feel the dawn of another era of our greatness,
      volcanoes of salt, sugar and spice,
      fire my spirit.

Now the ancients' drums thunder,
    the chorus of tongues untied
     sing of mankind's unbroken thread,
    chanting tomorrow is now.
    .

The winds rise, teasing my wings, lifting me,
     carrying me, returning me to the stars.

The breeze turns gusty,
    flatter my wings,
    back into the cosmos we return.

I Am A Butterfly

I am a butterfly

    coloured bright and true

    emotions of every hue

    beautiful,

    bind me

I bruise and die.

The Dance Of A Thousand Dances

In the wings I wait,

     waiting for my song.

I know my song is coming,

     after a while

     when all but one song is sung.

     that will be my song - the last song.

The beginning of my dance

     is in that last song,

     the dance of a thousand dances.

When I take center stage

     when the spotlight is on me,

     there will be no more worries,

     old fears I will trample under my feet,

     and the world will be at my fingertips.

When my song is sung.

     I will dance

     the dance of a thousand dances.

What Are We

We name black

    the colour of death

We name white

    the colour of witches and ghosts

We are neither black

    nor are we white

What are we?

The Struggle Is Over

It has been a long journey.
A journey I was never prepared for,
a journey that took me away from my abode,
    the place where my spirit resides.

My life has been a struggle,
    the struggle to find my way back
    from a sojourn of time taking its time,
    a long sojourn away from myself.

All these years in the wilderness of time,
    decades in bondage of time taking its time,
    time that was neither wasted nor harvested.

It was time captured in places where my soul was busy
    yet starved of the rhythm of life,
    the vibrations of the heart
    and the dreams of my mind.

Time, the invisible architect,
    stacked the years like heavy bricks around me,
    forging walls that grew thicker, heavier,
    harder to tear down.

I struggled mightily to divorce myself from
    the clutches of time taking its time,
    but time was the master, it continued to take its time.

Now time has released me.
I am back now.

I inhale the crisp air of the dawn,
     feeling its cool tendrils coil through my chest,
     chasing away the weight of long years.

Daily I breathe sighs of relief unbound by time.

My abode - my body,
     the place where my spirit resides,
     has survived my absence and neglect.

My eyes, the windows of my soul, have survived.
     but the cataracts of age,

     like gossamer veils

     give me a dim filtered view of the world outside

     blurring the once sharp edges of memory.

Now it is time for soap and water,
     wine and laughter,
     one for my body,
     and the other for my soul,
     to cleanse the painful weariness away from my body
     and banish the vacuum of the barren years from my soul.

Water strips away the dust of time;
     wine splashes warmth into the hollow spaces left behind.

My spirit has returned.

> I am with me again.

Like a wanderer stepping onto familiar soil,

> I feel my essence settle,
>> no longer a ghost drifting between lost years.

The struggle is over.

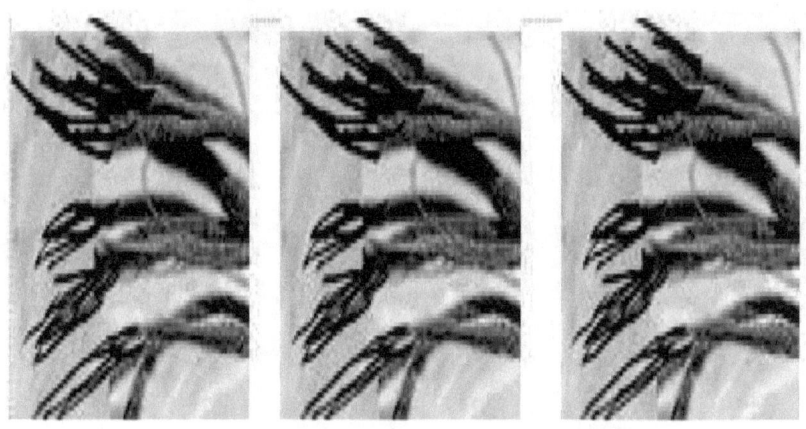

Arrested Departure

My ancestor's spirit
  hovered over my soul.

Where do you fly to in the dead of night?
He asked.

Away, away far from here,
  my soul cried.

My ancestor's spirit
  wiped the tears from my soul
  and suspended my flight.

I am still here.

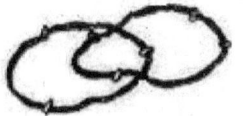

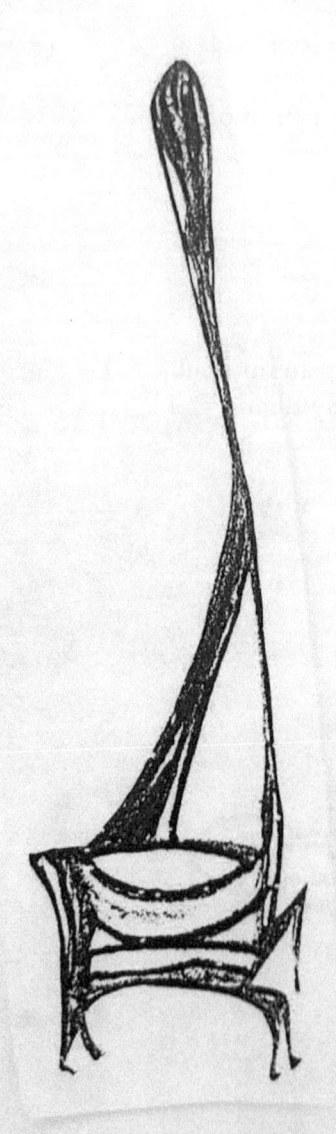

My Stool

In the circle of men
when I stand,
what is my stool?

What do I represent
that I sit on?

What is the name
that I carry,
the lode star of my people?

Do I bear any resemblance
to my ancestors,
whose honour and dignity
cultivated the genius of my father
and the grace of my mother?

Do I exude the fragrance of their sweet sweat
that baked in the African soil they cultivated
and watered the bountiful harvest of their fields
for me to be here today?

Does my voice throw into the heavens
in truth to power,
like the bellow of my grandfather's bull,
that roamed the cattle pens
and sired my inheritance -
the countless calves that became our livestock?

When I stand in the circle of men,
is my name
the same as the honour of my ancestors?

No Place To Be African and Free

Apartheid
Colonialism
Neo-colonialism
Slavery
Chattel Slavery
Colour Bar
Capital Punishment
Cultural Banishment
Jim Crow
Loss of Freedom
Loss of Life
Loss of Limbs
Loss of Vowels
Loss of nouns, adjectives, adverbs, proverbs
Loss of language
Chinua Achebe says
English is NOT an African language
Tell me about it
But English is the only language allowed
It is the story of my life
No Place to be African and free.

Sunday Morning in Harare

Quiet roads,
       petaled carpets
       of jacaranda purple,
       tranquil sunlight
       spackling in-between the jacaranda trees,
       you feel the cool morning breeze
       buzzing like jazz notes in the air,
       quiet and peaceful

it's Sunday morning in Harare.

Hell Is A Private Place

The body you see clothed
    so respectfully
    my head well groomed,

    the smile you admire so well
    my teeth bright as white,

    the civil words you hear
    my communication with you,

    is all there is for you.

I would not offend you with my odour
    affront your serenity with my frown
    nor disturb your tranquil neighbourhood
    with my painful screams,

    it is not for you.

The knots in my heart,
    the lumps in my throat
    the emptiness in my stomach
    are deep set silent partners of my life.

My blood has cuddled in my veins,

    of course,

None of this was meant for your ears.

Hell is a private place.

I Choose Peace

I choose peace.

The weight of sorrow presses deep,
a silent burden wrapped around my heart.
Only happiness washes away its gravity,
lifting the heaviness, unshackling the soul.

Happiness and sorrow,
        hand and glove,
never dwelling in the same space,
never touching at once.

They wait,
one lingering in the shadow of the other,
like dusk yielding to daylight,
one always retreating, one always arriving.

Yet peace is different,
 a meeting place
where light and darkness embrace,
where sorrow does not beg for relief,
where joy does not demand to reign alone.

Peace is harmony,
where the heart neither struggles nor surrenders,
where both pain and solace share the same breath.

Deep in my soul, I choose peace.

Nothing But Dust

I am earth
I am human
we are earth
mounds of sand,
dust, anthills, mountains,
fertile fields, barren fields,
plowed fields, fallow fields,
riverbeds, ocean beds, beaches,
rock, coal, gold, diamonds,
all dust
fat people, short people, tall people, skinny people,
yellow people, white people, brown people, black people,
pink people, purple people...
all dust, all earth,
one earth, one race
from dust
to dust.
We are
the human race.

My Life, A Walk After A Rainfall

Though my brow is furrowed deep,
       it carries no frown.
Though my hands are calloused and worn,
       they remain steady, gentle.
These marks, etched by time,
stand as quiet witnesses to its passage.

But my soul is serene.

My life is a walk upon the earth after the rain.

There were gentle showers, cool, cleansing.
There were torrents, thunder cracking,
rivers spilling over, leaving the fields drowning,
yet breathing new life into brittle roots.

And, of course, there were places where rain fell upon stone,
 where nothing ever grew.

Such is my life
       a walk upon the earth after a rainfall,
       where the water leaves its mark,
       whether in bloom or barren silence.

When I Leave This Place

Across the late afternoon sky,
a rainbow spills its breath in colour,
golden light retreats,
and the sky-dome rises,
stars parade in a luminous runaway,
each vying for brilliance in their celestial neighbourhood.

When I leave this place,
I too will be vying for brilliance in my neighbourhood.
I will go back to my own realm,
where my ancestors call my name.

My body you may burn or bury,
but I will not linger in the dust.
Like a tempest-born star tearing through the heavens,
I will rise, a luminous echo,
swallowed by the boundless ether,
where my ancestors stand,
not waiting,
but calling me home.

A Past Ever Present

Night pearls of laughter
from the bar across the street
sail into the empty night air
and land on my window sill.

Slowly they seep through the walls,
turning and churning these innocuous wisps of nocturnal reverie
into haunting ghoulish chatter
stirring my troubled sleep,
a sleep of unwelcome dreams,
dreadful vignettes of times past,
reminders of good times from by gone days,
good times turned bad.
The good times when such laughter like welcome rain
used to fill the barrels of my soul.

Now talking, then laughing,
the adulation and banter of the drunken bar patrons
wades wantonly through my head,
waking up the sleeping dogs of my past,
real monsters from a time of real pain,
when my world stopped
and I had to get off.

Each time the soundproof padded front door of the bar is opened,
the music from the jukebox
spills out onto the street,
vibrating discordant rhythms,
trumpets of terror,
and drums of thunder,
reminding me of flights
through the alleyways of my life,
where hordes of human jackals
chased me from home to here.

It is now 2AM
It is past closing time.

The bar falls deathly quiet.

The world exhales.

Now peace reigns on the street,
and sleep-
  sleep,
  beautiful sleep,
  finds me,
but only for now,
until tomorrow,

when visitations from beyond
will jar my sleep again

with a past ever present.

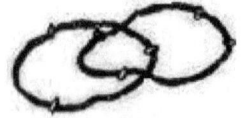

Where Is Here

Early dawn walking on the shoreline along the Atlantic Ocean,
I stop to look towards the east from whence I came.
The vastness of the celestial dome above me
and the boundless shimmering carpets of grey ocean waves
touching my feet below,
overwhelm me.

The faint nascent rays
of the day's sunlight,
comingling with the fading stars,
make eerie reflections
in the horizon
ignoring
my presence.

As the invisible curtain of the night
recedes to open up daylight,
I am gripped with loneliness
yet I feel that my insignificant presence
is at one with
all this spacious
space
earth
world
universe.

My mind wonders, gazing at the fading stars,
I know they shall return with the night.

They shall return as they always do,
because stars have a place.
The moon has a place.
The rivers, trees and even birds
have theirs,
natural places where they belong,
each contributing to the rhythm of life with their uses woven into
the quiet design of the universe,
an unseen note in the great symphony of time.

My mind wonders,
where is my own space,
the natural place
that is mine, where I belong;
like stars belong in the sky and the trees belong
in the land with the birds and the rivers?

Where is the space untouched by hands of decree,
where my being breathes as effortlessly as the stars claim the sky?
Where is my true place, not chosen for me by man or government,
where I simply belong, as purposefully as the stars in their sky?

The stars light the night sky
the birds spread seeds for new
trees to germinate and populate the land.
What about me?

What is my natural purpose?

I continued to gaze looking east as the
sun in all its golden glory began to emit

soft rays of shafts of light reflected on the ocean waters.
Beyond the horizon,
the sun was there and was surely coming at me,
but where was I?

I resumed my walk along the shoreline
lost in space, lost in mind,
was there any reason for me to be found?

Was there any reason
for my existence
written somewhere in a natural place
for me
and all the world
to see why I am here?

And even so,
where is here?

Time & Destiny

I am young
    only because
    my future lies ahead.

I have time
    only because
    my flowers need my hand.

I have a destiny
    only because
    my soul surges to go...

The Colour of Your God

What is the colour of your God?

> Is he blue eyed blonde
> is he Indian brown
> is he Congolese black
> or is he Eskimo alabaster white?

What is the colour of the mirror
> you look in?

Who shaped its reflection,
> whose hands turned glass into belief?

Do you dare trust that mirror you have been looking in?

Man fashions illusions,
> but rivers speak no lies.

Kneel at the water's edge,
where truth ripples in ancient tongues.

Look into the waters in the river,
what face stares back at you?

That face is the colour of your God.

Love Lost & Found

The lightness of you

The lightness of you is like a butterfly,
flying free in fields of flowers,
gently touching here
touching there
on the petals of my heart,
spreading joy and laughter
all over the land,
the harvest I treasure.

The lightness of you makes my heart flatter,
carrying me into heavenly surrender
mesmerized by your spirit,
the fount of banter and laughter
that leaves my face aglow.

The lightness of you brings peace to my heart,
a gentle breeze pregnant with seeds that quest for life,
searching for new daybreaks and new sunsets,
astral travel to the beginning of time
when it was all simple, all there, all natural.

The lightness of you opened the confluence of mine and yours,
spirits dancing in the flow and rhythm of life,

a prayer answered.

Smitten

I don't know
how you stoke the fire,
the warm glow you carry.

how you make the
world fall silent
to listen to your footsteps,

how you blossom
through all seasons,

how your eyes smile
even when it hurts,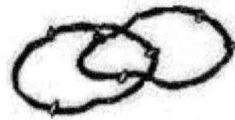

how your laughter
turns into melodious notes,

how your touch
makes it all seem alright.

I do know
I want to follow you
to unravel the mystery
you are
and wrap myself in it.

Perfect Release

Romance in the mind
        flights to never, never land
        easy and gracious

recollections of youth

        love and wonder

        release

        prefect capitulation

        brimful love

        passion's mentor

in the repose of a warrior

        cauldrons of anxiety boil

        under the fire of a thirst

        that's unquenchable

then peace in my heart

        the journey and trail

        beckon another tomorrow

        lay me down in the night.

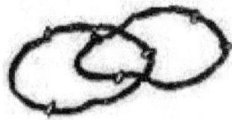

I Remember You

When I saw you

      our eyes danced together and filled a void we both carry,

      an echo answered.

Words tumbled out

      like the keys of a rusty old piano

      in tune but out of sync.

The words we spoke began to make music

      like a breeze that cooled a hot summer

      of a long time ago,

      a time sometimes remembered

      notes that brought the best of yesterday to today.

Like rain,

      your smile has come with words

      that give life to the seeds in my heart

      ready to grow.

I know we have met before

      in another life time

      when light dwelt in darkness

      when mountains were no more than dustbowls

      when oceans were no more than

      meandering rivers looking for a home.

when your soul roamed unbound,
a restless star drifting the celestial tide,
when your heart was a promise waiting to unfurl into
constellations.

I knew you then,

    when I too traveled with the wind and rain

    amid the virgin galaxies, single and free.

I remember you,

    do you remember me?

Impossible Life

The resonance of love notes,
a blood partnership of souls,
spirit of the same being
existing in two bodies.

One is here
the other is there,
but there
does not exist
because
there is here.

Like a circle,
its beginning is its end.
Its end is its beginning.
A circle of four hands
fingers intertwined.
lovers' legs
locked in rhythm.

A shared spirit
of two living as one.
Two sides of the same coin
living the impossible life.

I Stand and Ponder

I stand before you,

the door to your heart closed— but not locked.

I pause, uncertain.

Your laughter is warm,

your arms open,

the fire in your heart inviting.

Yet, still, I hesitate.

Joy fills the air, your spirit calls to me,

"Come closer."

Yet, still, I hesitate.

I ask myself, am I worthy?

To The Ocean

When destiny smiles on two

time becomes a river.

No matter

where it may be,

to the ocean

it will flow.

When two become lovers,

their love becomes

a boat on a river,

and

to the ocean

in love

it will flow.

Trepidation

She, who was with the celestial mist of creation,
   was my wife.

Called she was to bear five children with me,
   each for the five fingers
   that make the human hand,
   the human race.

In a dream, wrapped in starry darkness,
   in the chamber of the gods,
   she was presented to me.

She was woman, large of soul, sweet of heart.
She was night, the burning passion of creation.
She was day, the open cauldron of love.

Freely she was given,
   yet shackled she was by the frailty of flesh,
   chained to a million mortal mirages,
   illusions heavier than the mountains of the universe.

Still she carried herself with regal surrender
   among the mortals.

She came with the power of darkness,
   and to the night she would return,

leaving me each dawn,

lonely,

adrift in my chamber,

shattered, longing, unmoored.

I, free and unbound,
    rose to follow her,

      where sweet comfort in my arms, she would give.

Regal and serene, she stood at the threshold of my chamber,
    free of all the doors in my chamber,

      unfettered, untouchable,

      each door a path to her petaled feet my lips longed to kiss,
      each door dissolving into mist.

With morning dew on her lips
    and sweet sorrow in her eyes,

    she whispered

    soft as starlight,

    but loud as the heavens.
I bowed before her voice.

    "Trepidation," she whispered, *"Two stars we are, in splendid heaven we meet, but only by night can we ever be..."*

I, godly yet human,
    stood trembling in the glow of her departure.

The Memory of Your Face

In the quiet of the night
    in my fireplace
    lay light gray ashes
    encrusted with fading
    yellow reddish diamond nuggets.

In the embers of my dying fire
    there
    I see
    a faint glow of the memory of your face,
    a mirage in my mind.

It lingers on.

Your smile remains imprinted
    in the warm chambers of my heart.

Was it there all the time?

I do not remember.

Still, I see it,
    glowing and glowing
    circumscribing your face.

Still, it lingers on.

Waiting For Rain

Any thought of her

was a revelation across the landscape of his life.

The abundance of her spirit

and the grace of her laughter,

revealed the bareness of his own life,

a drought-stricken existence.

Any thought of her

whipped up the whirlwinds on the dusty plains of his life

and set him on the verge of tears,

tears he would welcome.

He lived, waiting for the cleansing waves of those tears,

the thunder that quickened his heart,

longing for her.

Each thought of her

was a revelation of the darkness in the chambers of his mind,

a dark and dormant place.

A place where he lived a life curled in a fetal posture,

a life without sinew,

waiting, waiting for her,

waiting for rain.

GRIOT

Griot

I sing this song
    I know no other.
My tongue, rich and exotic
      is rough and foreign.

I sing this song
     only I can sing it.
I am the griot of the family.
I sing of the scattered children of Africa
     dispossessed of the milk of their mother's breast
     and their father's heritage.

I sing this song
     because I hear the ocean's lament
     of people unburied in its belly.

I sing this song
     my bare feet walking this crusted bloody earth,
     hear the anguish of ancient tongues,
     talk of their horrible deaths
          for their land and labor,
     death without honor, without purpose.

I sing this song
     to jog your memory,
     to haunt your paradise.
I survived to sing it for all Africa.

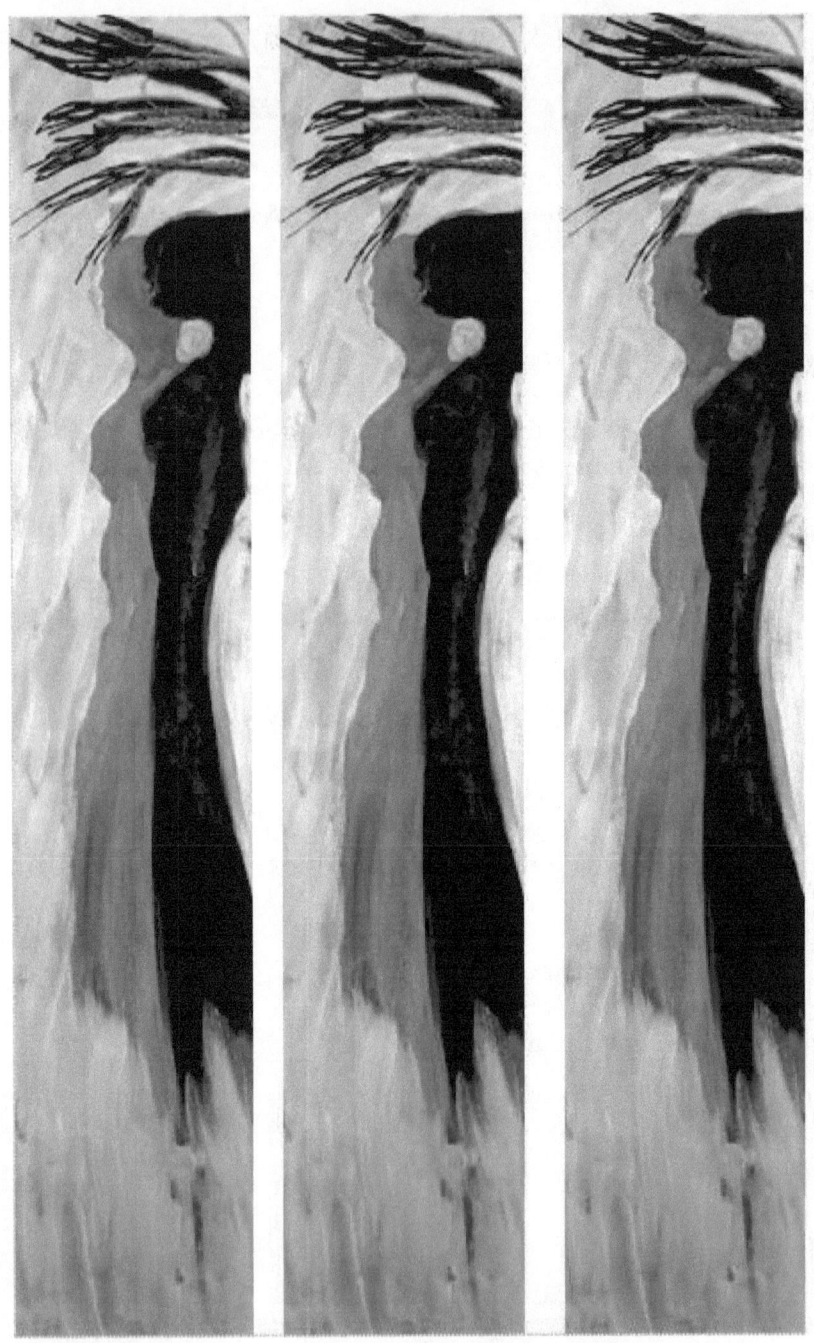

In The Ship's Hold

Blood curdling anguished screams
pierce the night
and shut out
the daylight.

The stench of feces
and urine
choke off all life.

And the ship sails on
to the New World.

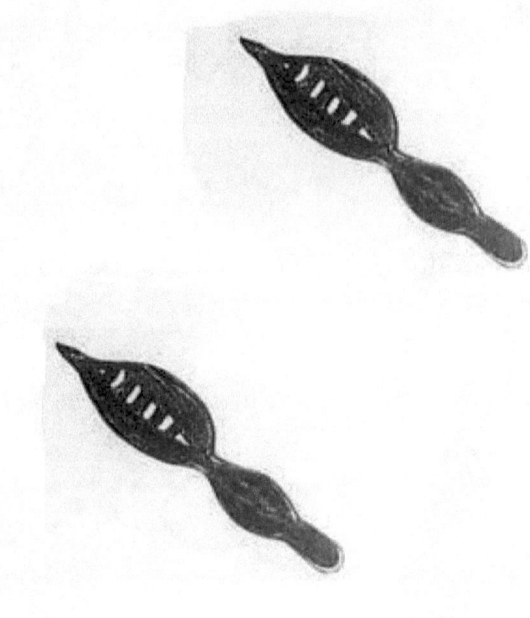

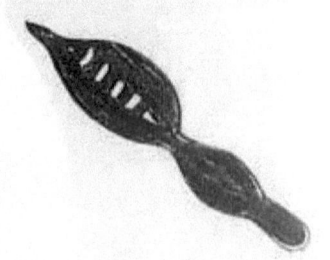

My Grandfather Called

My grandfather called

"I am coming", I said

and continued to play.

I was six.

He called me again.

"I'm coming", I said,

and I meant it,

but I had to finish my game.

I was twelve.

My grandfather asked me to sit down for a minute.

"As soon as I get back." I said.

but I did not come back then.

I was eighteen.

My grandfather is gone.

I wonder why he was calling me.

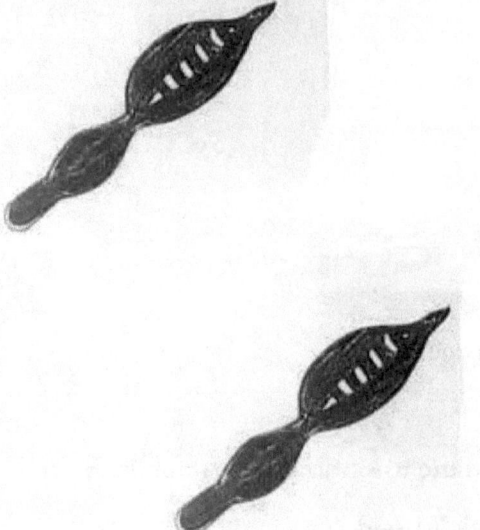

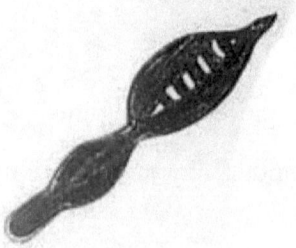

I Lost My Name

Mother let me sit down
but please
don't let go of my hand.

Like a fool at the marketplace,
I have lost my name.
The name you gave me.
I set it down
like an old hat,
some place,
somewhere,
sometime ago.
Now I don't remember my name.

Lulled and beguiled
by forbearers of foreign aid
and foreign religions,
purveyors
of progress and
civilization,
I am in the hypnotic grip
of electronic witches and wizards
from New York's Madison Avenue, London's High Street and China's Mandarin Central,
all beaming subliminal cultural seductions at me.

Subliminal seductions
to be this, to be that,
but not that.
Like a cat jumping to catch
sparks of light flashes on a wall,
I have become this,
I have become that, but not that.

Shaken hither and thither,
my native insight has lost its compass.
I am now a blind man,
because my eyesight is buried deep
in my lost insight.

Like a fool at the marketplace,
I have lost my name,
the name of my father.
My mind has travelled a twisted road,
chasing after gleaming starry shadows
and silhouettes of saints and godheads
seeking light
where there is darkness.
Now my eyesight serves me not
because my insight is buried in darkness.

Today a christian, tomorrow a muslim
maybe a buddhist or a hari krishna.
I have become all these things
yet I am not any of them.
I have brought home with me
languages that denigrate our creator
and shame your natural look,
leaving my name behind
like a fool at the marketplace.

Mother I am lost.
Do not let go of my hand.
Teach me who I am again.
Tell me my name again.
In my name is my past.
In my past is the mojo
wherein was created the dream
that I am,
an akhan, ashanti,, mandigo,

yoruba, igbo, kikuyu, masai,
mutonga, zezuru, xhosa, zulu,

but now I am none of me.

My heart and soul,
filled with fleeting, clashing images
of shadows and silhouettes
of things from cultures
borrowed and adopted
have rendered my god
impotent.
My eyesight has shut down
buried deep in my lost insight.

Mother hold my hand,
and take me back into your womb,
our land from whence we came,
the cauldron of our beauty,
our strength and our creativity,
so I can see again.

Unite As One

Africa, I pray that you will sail
past the these western horizons
past these eastern horizons
into the depths of the ocean
to emerge high above
with tomorrow's dawn
a new god
victor
over the pestilence
of oppression
exploitation
and ignorance
united
as one.

The Circle Is Complete

As the circle complete itself,
we levitate into another plane,
a consciousness of the self and society.

The spiritual spirals entwine
and ricochet off each other's nuclei.

The courses followed are parallel
and yet dissimilar,
and sometimes
it seems the africanness of one
is separate from the others,
a paradigm of mental differences,
the self mutating in one direction,
introspectively,
while society matures on its own
and seeks to reach the ideal for all.

But the loop comes around
for neither can exist in a vacuum
devoid of the other.

As the circle completes itself,
it obliterates from memory
the years of servitude
and decades of degradation.

All that remains
in the bedtime stories,
the epics
and the narratives,
are grandiose fairy tales,
narcissistic glorifications of the past
an Africa that might have been
a long time ago.

That glorious African past whose ethos is a flame
embodied in the triple coloured splendour
of a red, green and black rainbow
that fertilized
its dark thick African soil.

As the circle completes itself,
the scars left by the leg irons, the chains and handcuffs
on these ankles and wrists
seem to darken
and assume the natural hue of my Africa.

The bitterness and anguish,
the tears and bloody nightmares,
have mellowed
into the farthest recesses of the mind
like the timbre of a dying distant drum.

And to the children
the sun shines,
the moon calls the lovers,
they talk of tomorrow
in easy accents,
unhurried,
unperturbed
by the fading echo
of the crack of the slave driver's whip.

The circle is complete.

Home

Tell Africa, my friends
I have traveled
alone
so far into the darkness of Babylon
only because
Africa was home to go to.

I Dreamt in Swahili Last Night

I dreamt in Swahili last night.
In my ear cascaded melodious voices
in tongues that weave
the tapestry of Africa's breath,
whispers in Kikuyu and Asante Twi
from the Serengeti's chant to Sahara's hush.

I danced with daughters of the
Ibo, the Masai, the Akan, the Xhosa, and the Matonga,
celestial sisters crowned in dusk and flame.

I flew astride the Zimbabwe Bird,
gliding from the cradle of the Nile
to the roar of the Zambezi River,
from the blue hush of the Mediterranean
to Cape Agulhas
where oceans bow in greeting.

I held court beneath Mali's golden dusk
with Mansa Musa, regal in wisdom's flame.
King Chaka-Zulu offered thunder-laced counsel,
while Munhumutapa traced legacy in the stars,
and the spirit of Sundiata Keita draped my shoulders
with benedictions like woven sun and ancestral dust.

Nubian maidens, veiled in ebony grace,
descended with drums echoing Songhai skies,
and in their bridal dances, memories bloomed.

Royalty of the east and the west exchanged crowns.
The south and the north met as siblings beneath the baobab.

A continent risen in regal unity.

I dreamt in Swahili last night,
and sang in Yoruba tones,
praises blooming in every name.

Africa, cradle of light.
Africa, mother of might.
Africa, forever crowned.

Vignettes Of War

For those who made the ultimate sacrifice that I may be a free African man in my own country, among them my brothers Richard, Dennis and Biggie fallen heroes of our struggle for independence.

Our African Future: sand, glass, and mirrors

I was not in our future
neither was my brother.

I died somewhere between the day I was born
and the day I left home to go America
to seek peace in my world.

My brother died somewhere between the night
he boarded the train to Mozambique to go to war
and the day they announced
the end of all wars.

We traveled together to our African future as brothers
but we lived our lives as strangers.

We suffered the same pain
but survived it differently
and died of it separately.

All across the continent
the rapacious European colonial beast
rampaged among us
pillaging our souls.

Undaunted was my warrior brother
he mounted the wild beast
and rode it
until it frothed at the mouth
and bled from its flanks.

Civilized I was,
>   standing in its crazed path
>   in suit and tie,
>   I called for peace.

I was trampled under.

I did not die then
>   I only suffered permanent mental
>   and physical disfigurement.

We lived together on the road to our future
>   my brother and I,
>   he, riding the obstinate beast
>   I, walking on foot
>   leery of the wild beast.

We traveled for years untold
>   yet our destination
>   was never anywhere in sight.

Those we met coming from our future
>   said they had seen it
>   but none would tell us exactly what it was.

I suspected they had never got there.

We traveled in the snow capped lands
>   of foreign people the likes of whom
>   no African had ever seen.

We met black people, brown people, yellow people
>   white people and even blue people.

We met them all on our journey to our future, they
spoke with us but
       I suspected they never said anything to us.

Tired and weary,
       we came upon a water well.
       We rested
       while my brother cleansed my calloused bleeding feet.

Ride on the beast behind me,
       my brother implored.

I refused.

I suspected it would kill me.

We traveled through myriad cities with temples
       built of glass and mirror.

Our reflections were in the glass and mirrors,
       and our images were inside the temples
       but we never entered the temples.

We came to the edge of the cities,
       it was desert
       long endless desert.

My brother said
       I have tamed the wild beast,
       now let us remain in the cities
       our images are already here.

I refused.
       I was determined to continue to our future.

He begged me to stay in the cities
      where our images were.

Steadfastly
      I refused.

In parting
      he gave me the tamed wild beast
      to take me to our future.

I bid him farewell
      and rode the tamed wild beast.

I traveled the length and breath of the deserts
      there was no end to the emptiness and the sand.

Eventually
      I grew weary and laid in the sand.

When I awoke
      my image was in the sand.

I looked for the tamed wild beast
      it had disappeared in the sand of the desert.

I walked in aimless wonder
      searching for the road to our future
      until I found myself in the myriad cities again.

I found my brother,
      in his eyes was the glass and mirrors
      of the temples.

I saw my image reflected from him
  but I was not in him.

He rushed to greet me.

I gave him my hand
  but it turned to sand.

We begun our journey from our future
  my brother and I,
  but I suspected we had already died,
  he, in the image of glass and mirrors,
  I, in the sands of the endless desert.

...a shameless, desolate, hungry present

He looked around him,
the deflected sunlight in the cave
reflected a dim luminescence on the rock walls of
the cave.

The air was cool and dry.

Fifteen weary men lay sprawled
on the dirt floor,
each lost in his own fantasy of
what food and
clean water tasted like.

Each fighting his own war with
his own stomach.

Their eyes may have been
closed
        but a man can only
sleep so much.
Their armor stood silent guard
against the rock
walls staring with pity at these desperate
        would-be masters.

He crawled to the mouth of the cave.

He thought he had felt a twinge in his bowels
     to relieve himself.
No one paid him any attention.

He was a leader with nothing to give,
     a ghost that had used up all its heavenly favors.
They knew he was as hungry as they were
     and surely,
      if he had the power of *Chaminuka.*
he would have turned stone into bread by now.

He was just a man,
     there was no point in taunting him with the fact.
He stuck his head out of the cave.

The laser sharp rays of the hot afternoon sun
     hit his eyes.

He searched for the man on sentry duty.
He saw him.

He was sitting fifty yards away under a tree
     that had lost its dignity as a tree
     when it lost its conception
     of what a tree is supposed to be.

It was leafless.

Its limbs stood out like bundled turfs of hair
     on the head of a demented person.

He waved at the sentry.

The sentry waved back with the slightest
     movement of a finger.

The hot dry sun had sapped all his energy.

He wondered over to the huge dead msasa tree
     on the other side.

He stood under the tree.

The guerrilla warfare-trained animal instinct in him scanned
     the rock outcrops around the dead tree and
     the desert like terrain in its perimeter
     and beyond.

His hand casually caressed
     the butt of the ak47 assault rifle on his shoulder.

His mind absorbed the topography of the area
     comparing what he saw

with something already stored in his mind.

Everything was still.

No man dared the insufferable heat.

The beasts of the forests had long gone.
and the flies had fled underground.

A large solitary lizard was the exception.

It sunbathed itself, on what,
      he vividly imagined,
      was a hot burning rock.

It seemed suspended between
      the oppressive scorching rays of the sun and
      the baking hot reflective surface of the rock.
      had it not been for the regular respiratory
      movement under its thorax,
      he would have presumed it dead.

He turned his eyes to the sky shielding them
      with his open hand.

From far away

i heard the anguished cry of a newborn baby.

it was the cry of afrika's man-child on its first instance on earth.

i shook my head in sorrow,

because it was too late then.

his umbilical cord had been severed and buried.

i shouted into the wind and admonished him

"You cannot go back into your mother's womb.

You are on your own,

son of the soil..."

(continued over leaf)

Hither and thither
>
> bleached dry broken animal bones
>
> lay forlorn on the cracked hard earth
>
> bearing miserable testimony
>
> to the life that had once encased them.

The rivers that had run with vivacious fury
>
> through the valleys
>
> had turned into gaping gullies
>
> broad meandering sandy furrows
>
> that looked
>
> ugly and purposeless.

His fingers fumbled over the pockets of his dirty shirt
>
> and found a pinch of dry coarse tobacco
>
> and a piece of an old newspaper.

Mechanically,
>
> he began to roll himself a cigarette.

> He patted his pockets for matches.
>
> He went through his fatigues,
>
>> pocket by pocket.
>
> He did not find the accursed matches.

His evil filled eyes stared at the crudely rolled cigarette,
    and cursed it silently,
    throwing it away.

Slowly, he lowered himself down,
    and slumped under the tree.
    His scuffed boots
    dug into the hard dry soil for support.

He searched hopelessly in the sky
    for a cloud,
    even a speck of a cloud.

His faltering belief argued with his sanity,
    surely there used to be a life giving
    tropical rain from that same sky.

Or was his mind deranged?

For the sake of his sanity,
    his eyes searched again,
    every where,
    searching for anything,
    any kind of sign to reassure him
    that he had not been transported

unconsciously

by some conjuration of the white man

or by some quirk of evil fate

been transported to another time

another place

another country

a desolate, god forsaken, barren no man's land.

He needed a reaffirmation

    that this was still the same country

    that his ancestors had bequeathed him.

    That this was the same country

    they had shed their blood in

    to fertilize its soil for his seed.

Hs heart longed for the spittle

    from a mother's lips to her sickly child.

Will you mother fornicating sky, please tell me,

    is this the same country

    that we have become orphans for,

    fair game to the guns of war

    and the incisor of the nocturnal hyena?

Is this the land of our forefathers' graves

> or is it

> a treacherous harlot of the yellow bearded

> white man?

Have the spirits of our ancestors lost

> yet another battle to the white man's foreign gods?

Answer me!

Do you hear me, you mother fornicating sky?

There was no answer.

His remonstrations went the way of the wind.

He was met by the stare of an ungodly, vacant

> celestial dome.

> It had no interest in him,

> just as it had no interest in the patched earth

> he was sitting upon.

In all directions

> the empty sky stretched into the horizons

> dragging sheets,

> upon shimmering sheets of heat waves

> that scotched the brown earth in their wake.

The world had become a shadowless wasteland.

> The grass had died and withered
>
> into chaff in the wind.

Bark stripped trees stood

> like shameless dismembered human figures, dead
>
> and improperly interned in grotesque upright
>
> > caskets.

He tried to think

> but no thought had enough power to firmly
>
> grip his mind.

A myriad curses found favor with his tongue

> curses upon the sun
>
> for its heartlessness, and curses upon the earth
>
> for its cowardly surrender.

However, he soon ran out of strength,

> his extortion, the curses, and threats on the
>
> sun and earth went the way of the wind.

He just sat there, indolent.

Even the prime mover,

> the thought that he had wanted to relieve himself,
>
> the thought which had brought him here
>
> to the huge dead msasa tree
>
> to relieve himself
>
> was now too weak to push him into the action.

Like the man on sentry duty
      he sat under the tree that had lost
      its conception of what a shade was supposed to be.

His hands groped the ground aimlessly.
      They found a twig and broke it in two.
      and threw it away.

His tortured soul and his troubled mind
      irritated his body.

Seasoned by the years of the hard war he lived,
      his body froze and ignored the heat of the sun,
      and the rough pressure of the dry bark
      of the dead tree on his back.

Like the lizard on the hot baking rock
      he was suspended against the tree.

With each measured breath,
      the warm air circulated through
      his broad African nose and
      into his blood like an opiate.

Time went by in no particular sequence,
      it had no direction either.

Time and mind had wed.

> Their wedding bed was now hovering above
>
> in the dry empty sky
>
> knowing not
>
> whether to leap into some glorious
>
> illusionary future
>
> or to return to the familiar hounds of yesterday,
>
> through the valleys of often re-lived triumphs
>
> and gullies of painful
>
> but time cured memories.

The present,

> this wretched offspring of an apathetic god,
>
> this indubitable testament
>
> of human impotence
>
> in the face of a deaf and hostile natural force,
>
> he banished away,
>
> locked it in its own infernal ignominy
>
> as another familiar past
>
> endured and conquered,
>
> until
>
> it too
>
> was suspended.

The wonderous union of time and his mind

    eloped to his yesterdays,

    his childhood,

    his political puberty

    and maturity.

In the crevices of his yesterdays

    he hoped

    the union would find and bring to the present

    some semblance of logic

    some purchase

    that could possibly justify

    this shameless, desolate, hungry present.

In Memoriam

Tribute to the unknown young refuegee-turned-freedom-fighter who survived the raid of the camp in Mozambique.

Massacre at Nyadzonya

Inspired by August 1976, Ian Smith's Rhodesia Government forces raid and massacre of helpless refugees at Nyadzonya Refugee Camp, Mozambique.

The massacre brought the immediate ruthlessness of the war home to him and the few fortunate survivors of the raid.

They had left Rhodesia with an ideal to free themselves and the country, however, that ideal was potentially nothing but sentiment.

The mental and emotional perspectives he had held of death were those of teenagers who had attended funerals of relatives and the relatives of friends. The kind of death he had known and experienced in his young life in that regard was the cushioned death that comes from old age, sickness and occasionally, a motor vehicle accident. That death explained itself and even confirmed the dynamic of life. It was death that brought people together and solidified their will to live life, not only their own, but that of the departed.

The death that the massacre brought to him had no dynamic of life nor any philosophical explanation. It was death that had no end other than itself. The eight hundred people who had died, died without the dignity of old age, sickness or even an accident. The dead were dead without the honor of a personal death as their birth had been. They had died like animals of the jungle; their lives would be missed by no one and their death would have no wake. Their relatives wherever they were in Rhodesia would not know of their death; even if they did, no one would even pose to reflect upon their departure. Indeed, they had in a way ceased to exist when they became refugees in Mozambique. The pictures of their dead bodies would appear in the newspapers and on television screens, but no one would know who they were. They were all dead Africans, who belonged in their death. Those Africans in Rhodesia who were alive to see the pictures of their dead fellow Africans could only store the images of their death deep in the folds of their own dead lives. The business on hand was to be alive not dead.

The young man did not know what to do with the death that had pervaded his mind.

He could not mourn for eight hundred people. The weight of their dead bodies was to heavy to bear, however, neither could he put it down. Deep within him, he groped in the darkness of death and despair searching for a bridge, a ladder to carry him out of the mass grave he was stuck in.

Vengeance, savage raw vengeance, massaged his heart and brought a light into his eye. Political and military arguments were no more than philosophical platitudes. They could not bare the brutal sadistic death he had lived through. His wide dark nostrils stank of blood and burning flesh.

His vision was invaded by flashes of gruesome pictures of any one of the scenes of the massacre he had witnessed and lived through. How do you bury eight hundred bodies? No piece of earth was large enough to swallow them and flower.

However, he was alive. In that insanity that he lived in, he was separate from those who had died. Death in this animal fashion that it had come in could possibly return and finish him and whoever else had survived. He had to live, to stop that death. He would not die. He felt a surge of omnipotence.

He had defied and hidden from death.

He would live and outwit death again.

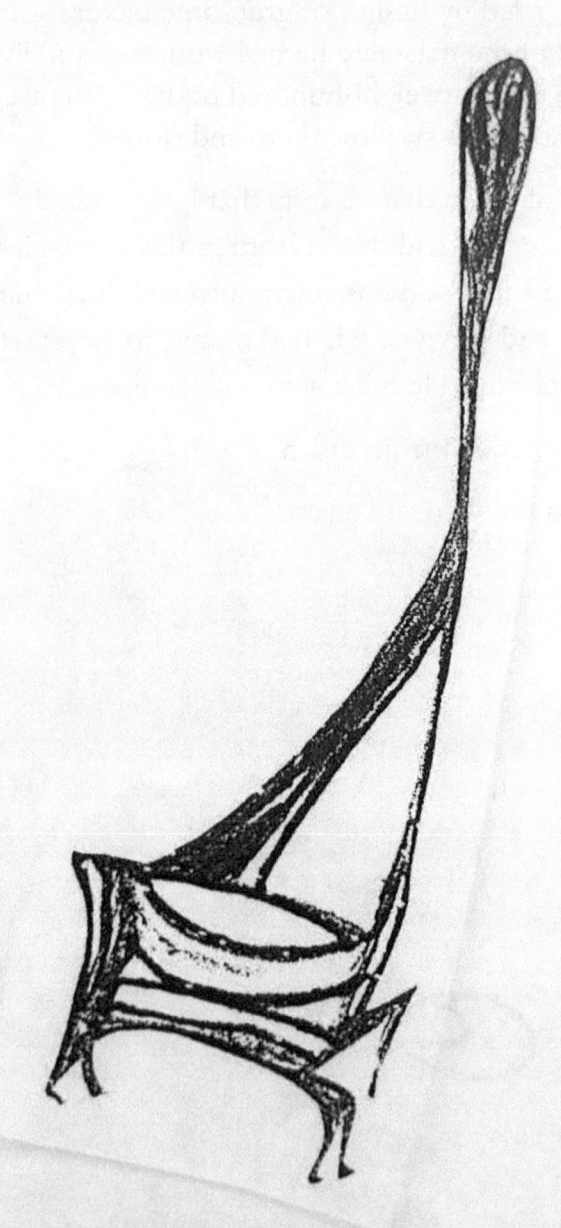